Praying Lent

*Renewing Our Lives on the
Lenten Journey*

Loyola Press *in partnership with* Creighton University's
Online Ministries

Praying Lent

Renewing Our Lives on the Lenten Journey

Andy Alexander, SJ
Maureen McCann Waldron

LOYOLA PRESS.
A JESUIT MINISTRY
Chicago

LOYOLA PRESS.
A JESUIT MINISTRY

3441 N. Ashland Avenue
Chicago, Illinois 60657
(800) 621-1008
www.loyolapress.com

In accordance with c. 827, since this material has been found free from doctrinal or moral error, permission to publish in the Archdiocese of Chicago has been granted by the Very Reverend John F. Canary, Vicar General, on September 17, 2008. Permisssion to publish does not imply that the one granting this permission agrees with the content, opinions, or statements expressed therein. Nor is any legal responsibility assumed by the Archdiocese of Chicago by granting this permission.

The material in this book was developed for and originally appeared on Creighton University's Online Ministries Web site Praying Lent (www.creighton.edu/CollaborativeMinistry/Lent/).

Scripture texts in this work marked as NAB are taken from the *New American Bible with Revised New Testament and Revised Psalms* © 1991, 1986, 1970 Confraternity of Christian Doctrine, Washington, D.C. and are used by permission of the copyright owner. All Rights Reserved. No part of the *New American Bible* may be reproduced in any form without permission in writing from the copyright owner.

Scriptures marked as CEV are taken from the *Contemporary English Version* Copyright © 1995 by American Bible Society. Used by permission.

Cover design by Judine O'Shea and Beth Adler
Interior design by Beth Herman

Library of Congress Cataloging-in-Publication Data
Alexander, Andy.
  Praying Lent : resources to give life to our Lenten journey / Andy Alexander, Maureen McCann Waldron.
     p. cm.
  ISBN-13: 978-0-8294-2857-5
  ISBN-10: 0-8294-2857-7
  1. Lent. I. McCann Waldron, Maureen. II. Title.
  BV85.A44 2009
  263'.92—dc22
                                                        2008038281

Printed in the United States of America
09 10 11 12 13 14 15 Bang 10 9 8 7 6 5 4 3 2 1

Contents

Preface

We have called these reflections for Lent *Praying Lent* to emphasize that Lent is all about prayer. As we will see, prayer is about our relationship with God. Lent offers us a special opportunity to grow in our relationship with God and to deepen our commitment to a way of life that is rooted in our baptism. In our busy world, Lent allows us to reflect on our patterns, to pray more deeply, to experience sorrow for what we have done and what we have failed to do, and to be generous to those in need. We offer resources here to assist our entry into this wonderful season, from preparing for Lent to celebrating the holy three days at the end of Lent.

These reflections are made in the context of Ignatian spirituality. Ignatius of Loyola (1491–1556) was a Spanish noble who experienced a life-transforming conversion during which our Lord called him to be his companion in sharing Jesus' own mission from the Father. Ignatius's spirituality, developed while he was a layperson, is deeply rooted in real life. In his time, for laypeople who could afford the time, to grow in holiness almost inevitably meant spending lots of time in prayer. For religious it meant joining a monastery or convent. Ignatius found a way to describe a contemplative life for ordinary, busy people. Ignatius emphasized finding God in all things, and he called this process "dying to self," which leads to our becoming contemplatives in action.

This type of spirituality and these reflections on being intimate with our Lord during Lent recognize the need for self-knowledge, the presence of God's grace, and the purification of our desires. The practices that are outlined here for a powerful experience of Lent are all about the renewal and deepening of our desires, which lead to new hearts and ultimately to new behaviors and a freer following of our Lord.

These reflections are a print version of some of the Praying Lent material published on the Online Ministries Web site at Creighton University (www.creighton.edu/Collaborative Ministry/online.html). Many people from all over the world have requested permission to copy parts of the Praying Lent site for their parish, adult-formation programs, Rite of Christian Initiation of Adults candidates and catechumens, or prayer groups. Others have simply wanted to hold this kind of material in their hands, carry it with them on a trip, or have it near their bed stand.

We are grateful to Loyola Press for imagining this material in print and for producing it in a format that is so readily available to parishes and just about anyone looking for support during Lent. Loyola Press is planning to print the Daily Lent Prayer from the Praying Lent site. This collection of daily prayers for each day of Lent will be a wonderful companion to these resources.

—Andy Alexander, SJ
Maureen McCann Waldron

1

This Lent Will Be Different

Anything Worth Doing Is Worth Preparing For

Imagine that this Lent is going to be different from every other Lent we've experienced. Think about the many graces that are offered to us this year. Let's even imagine that God is going to help transform our lives, leading us to greater freedom, greater joy, and deeper desire for love and service.

If We Want It, We Will Choose It

Lent will be a wonderful season of grace for us if we give ourselves to it. And we will give ourselves to it if we want it badly enough. In these days before Lent, we need to prepare our hearts. We can do so by realizing how much we want to grow in freedom, how much we need to lighten our spirits and experience real joy, and how much some parts of our lives really need changing.

Preparing our hearts is a process of preparing our desires. This means practicing a sense of anticipation. If I imagine Lent as an "ordeal" or a time I dread in some way, then I've already predisposed myself to not get very much out of it. The days before Lent are a time to anticipate something wonderful that is about to happen.

Our Focus: What God Wants to Give Us

Our sense of excitement and anticipation will grow more easily if we begin to imagine what God wants to give us. Something is coming that we can truly look forward to. If we focus too much on what we are going to do or not do, we risk missing out on the gift God wants to give us. Lent is about God's great desire to bless us. All grace comes from God and is, therefore, God's gift. It is given to us to free us to love others as our Lord has loved us. What we want is to receive what God wants to give us.

Don't Start from a Dead Stop

Taking some time to get ready for Lent ensures that we don't miss the first week or two of Lent because we are just getting started. Lent begins on Ash Wednesday, but we want to be ready on that day and not just begin to think about Lent on that day. Part of what makes a vacation or an anniversary so special is the buildup, the anticipation.

Before Ash Wednesday, we should start asking ourselves some questions and begin making some preparations. Each of us can ask ourselves, *What does God want to give me this year? What will free me to be more open and more loving this year?* These questions may require that I slow down a bit and listen to my inner spirit. For example, even if I'm very busy, I realize I'm hungry when I hear my stomach start growling. Or we can ask, *What am I going to be doing on Ash Wednesday?* Too often, Ash Wednesday is like every other day, except that we manage to get to church to have ashes put on our forehead. Ask: Is there anything else I can do on Ash Wednesday? How will fasting and abstaining happen for me, for my family, on that special day?

Lent Is Not Something to Do Alone

With our spouses, children, close friends, and distant e-mail companions we can begin to talk about how we will support one another in this Lenten journey. Our anticipation and preparation are transformed in the companionship of family and friends. We shouldn't be deterred by the fear that others won't be "into" Lent. Jesus said, "Fear is useless; what is needed is trust." Let's begin now to tell others about our desires. Let's help support others' expectations. Let's help others see that Lent doesn't have to be something we avoid and that it certainly can't be reduced to giving up candy. We can help our loved ones begin to imagine what they can receive from God in these days.

A great place to start our planning is Ash Wednesday. Ash Wednesday is a day of fasting and abstinence. We can think about what we are going to eat on Ash Wednesday. We shouldn't be embarrassed if we haven't fasted in a long time or even ever before. We can plan to intentionally have only one full meal on Ash Wednesday. We can make that meal meaningful and symbolic, as this book will demonstrate later.

Getting Our House Ready

In the days before Lent, the resources here can give us concrete ideas of ways to get ready. We will explore a number of ways we can enter Lent with our whole selves, as body-persons, using our senses to help us experience things deeply. The symbols in our home and the choices we make can shape the way we will begin Lent as individuals and with our family.

It Doesn't Take Much Time

It doesn't take a lot of time to prepare for Lent. It just takes desire and focus. God can do so much with our hearts when they are focused. We can give God more space to touch our hearts if we begin to establish some simple patterns. For example, we can wake up each morning and stand by the edge of our beds for a few moments to ask the Lord for the grace to let this day be one in which we long for the beginning of Lent. Our prayer might be general, or we might pray for specific helps or graces for getting ready to begin Lent.

Whatever we say, our Lord understands our words. We can make this simple connection with God in the time it would take us to put on our slippers. Similarly, we can spend a short time in prayer each night giving thanks to God before we go to bed. This pattern of simple morning and evening prayer can stir our spirits to look forward to and prepare for Lent as a season of grace.

May our Lord bless us all on this journey ahead.

2

God's Invitation

Lent is a season of being invited by God in a deeply personal way. "Come back to me, with all of your heart," our Lord beckons (see Joel 2:12). "We will," we respond, but we aren't quite ready; our hearts are not prepared. We want to squirm, evade, avoid. We note that our souls are not yet perfect. We think we are not ready for God to love us.

Yes, of course I want to have a deeper relationship with God, we tell ourselves earnestly. And we will . . . soon. God calls to us again: "Come back to me, with all of your heart."

OK, OK, we think, *I really will. There are just a few more things I need to do at work. Let me spend a little more time in prayer first. Let me get to reconciliation. Let me clean my oven, tidy my closets. Let me sell the yoke of oxen, check on the field I have purchased. . . .*

Return to Me with Your Whole Heart

From the first day of Lent, the Ash Wednesday readings make God's call to us clear: "Return to me with your whole heart" (Joel 2:12 NAB). It is an extraordinary invitation from God to each one of us—to *me* in a personal, individual way.

God invites me to drop the defenses that I hold up between myself and God.

God wants us to realize that our standards, our ways of judging and loving, are very different from God's way, and so much smaller. God loves each one of us. For an entire Lenten season, for an entire lifetime, God loves each one of us.

"A clean heart create for me, God," Psalm 51:12 NAB offers. "Give me back the joy of your salvation." That is exactly what our loving God wants to give us, the joy of salvation.

In North America, Lent falls in the winter, and winter days are cold and dark, perfect for hiding ourselves indoors, perfect for hiding from God—or so we imagine. But our God is insistent, loving, gently prodding. God is the parent of the prodigal son, waiting faithfully and eagerly on the road for our return, night after night. There are no folded arms or stern judging stares, only the straining eyes of a parent ardently waiting for our return, longing to embrace us and rejoice in us.

Yet we spend so much time thinking about how to return and what to say, how to begin the conversation with God. It's only when we finally appear, embarrassed and confused, after so much time away, that we realize we don't have to say anything. We only have to show up.

Look to the road ahead: our loving God is jumping up and down for joy. We've heard the invitation to us. We have returned home!

But, wait . . . something stops us from this great reunion. What keeps us from accepting this invitation to something deeper in our lives with God? We feel that there are things we should say first: "Wait . . . but . . . if only." And finally, "If God really knew about me . . ."

It doesn't matter. The only reality is the joy that comes from returning to God, the joy we experience when God, like a loving parent, smothers us with embraces and joyful cries. We have returned!

Our acceptance of this call, this appeal to our hearts, is simple if we can only get beyond the fear. All we have to do is say to our Lord, "I'm here. Where do I start? Yes, I want to be with you." Our hearts have been opened, and we have taken the first step toward our rejoicing parent on the road. No explanations are necessary. We must only pause and picture in our hearts the joyfully loving and unblinking gaze of God that falls on us.

What's the next step on our journey home? We can take the earliest moments of our day, before we have gotten out of bed, to thank God for such a loving invitation and to ask for help in opening our hearts to it. We can remember throughout the day the invitation that has moved our hearts: "Come back to me, with all of your heart." We can rejoice along with God.

This is the invitation of each day of Lent. Today is the day to accept it.

3

What Needs to Change?

Expecting Different Results

The saying "Insanity is defined as doing the same thing over and over again, expecting different results," commonly used in twelve-step programs, can help us as we look at the choices for the days ahead. It is very simple: our Lord is calling us to a change of heart. We know from experience that nothing will change unless we change our patterns of behavior. To expect different results is insanity.

What Needs Changing?

We discover what needs changing by asking for help. We can simply pray, "Lord, help me to know what you want to change in me." This is one of those requests that God will surely answer. We ask for help; then we listen. It is often said that we must be careful what we ask for. With a little reflection, most of us will find ordinary habits and ways of being and acting that we aren't very proud of. We think of things we do and things we never get around to doing. We can feel the call to change our attitudes, our self-absorption, or our way of interacting with others. We reflect: Perhaps a spouse, a loved one, a friend, a family member, a coworker has told me something about myself that gets in the way of communication, that makes relating to him or her difficult. Maybe I don't take God very seriously. I go to church on Sunday, and contribute my share, but I don't really take time to deal with my relationship with God. Perhaps I've let my mind and imagination become cluttered with escapist litter. I might recognize self-indulgent habits. I may realize that I rarely, if ever, hear the cry of the poor and answer it. Perhaps dishonesty on many levels has become a way of life. One of the roadblocks in my relationship with God and others may be a deep wound or resentment from the past, something I continue to hold against others or myself.

Psalm 51 offers guidance for prayer:

> You are always merciful! Please wipe away my sins.
> Wash me clean from all of my sin and guilt.
> (Psalm 51:1–2 CEV)

Beginning New Patterns during Lent

Something all of us can do is commit ourselves to being more reflective during Lent. We can simply make a point of being more observant, more aware of what we're experiencing, more cognizant of our automatic behavior. We can then start paying attention to our many desires. During Lent, we can examine these desires and see which of them we need to purify, which we may need to abandon, and which are positive desires that we need to act on. Naming our deepest desires will guide the choices we make to establish new patterns for Lent.

Praying

Lent is the time to start new patterns of prayer. If we haven't been praying at all, this is a great time to begin. It is important to begin realistically. We can start by simply pausing in the morning upon rising, taking a slow, deep breath, recalling what we have to do this day, and asking for the grace to do it as a child of God. We might decide to go to bed a half hour earlier and rise a half hour earlier to get time alone for the readings for the day or some other devotion. Daily Mass is another choice. We might get to church fifteen minutes earlier each Sunday to reflect a bit. We can start a Lenten journal to record our reflections, our desires, and the graces we have received.

Eating

Lent is a great time to change our eating patterns. This is not about losing weight or getting in shape, though paying attention to what we eat should make a difference in our overall health. This is about being more alert. Anyone who has tried to diet knows that something changes in our mind when we restrict food. The ancient desert monks discovered that fasting heightened their consciousness. Not only did their bodies go on alert but also their whole person seemed to be in a heightened state of attention. Fasting aided prayer. It made it easier to listen to God more openly, especially in times of need.

For Catholics, only Ash Wednesday and Good Friday are required fast days. The requirement is simply to abstain from meat and eat one full meal on those days, with the other two meals combined not equaling a full meal. On the Wednesdays and Fridays of Lent, we may want to try to fast intentionally. Health permitting, we might try to eat very little, such as some juice or perhaps a small amount of beans and rice. We will experience how powerfully open and alert we feel and how much easier it is to pray and to name our deeper desires. We are likely to feel freer and more energized, less sluggish and tired.

The other advantage of fasting is that it is a simple gesture of solidarity with the poor of the world, who often eat little more than rice and beans each day. Powerful things happen in us when we think about those people in the world who have so much less than we do. Eating in solidarity with the poor is a great cure for self-pity.

Practicing Generosity

Almsgiving has always been an important part of Lent. Lent begins with the powerful reading from Isaiah 58:10–11 NAB on the Friday and Saturday after Ash Wednesday.

> If you bestow your bread on the hungry
> and satisfy the afflicted;
> Then light shall rise for you in the darkness,
> and the gloom shall become for you like midday;
>
> Then the lord will guide you always
> and give you plenty even on the parched land.
> He will renew your strength,
> and you shall be like a watered garden,
> like a spring whose water never fails.

Fasting and almsgiving foster generosity. Generosity is not as simple as giving excess clothing to a place where poor people might purchase them or writing a check to benefit the poor. These are wonderful practices. However, generosity is an attitude. It is a sense that no matter how much I have, all that I have is a gift, and given to me to be shared. It means that sharing with others in need is one of my personal priorities. This is quite different from assessing all of my needs first and then giving away what is leftover. A spirit of selfless giving means that one of my needs is to share what I have with others.

Lent is a wonderful time to practice selfless giving because it takes practice. Self-sacrificing generosity is a religious experience. It places us in solidarity with the poor who share with one another without having any excess. It also joins us with Jesus, who gave himself completely for us. Establishing new patterns of giving will add real life and joy to Lent.

Practicing Penance

Part of the healing process for sprained ankles might involve physical therapy. The injured ankle is tender and swollen. I might put ice on it to reduce inflammation, wrap it, elevate it, and stay off of it. Later I will start moving it and walking on it. Eventually, as the injury heals, I will start exercising it so that it will be stronger than it was before and I won't injure it again.

That healing process is similar to penance. Penance is spiritual therapy for the healing we desire. The Lord always forgives us, without condition. But complete healing takes time. With sins or bad habits we have invested years in forming, we need to develop a therapeutic plan of care to let the healing happen. To say "I'm sorry" or to simply resolve to change without taking specific steps to act differently is not enough. It's like continuing to walk on a sprained ankle while wishing it would heal.

Lent is a wonderful time to name the sinful, unhealthy, self-centered patterns that need changing and to act against them by coming up with a strategy of healing. When the Lord shines light into the darkness of a bad pattern, the first step is to choose to stop that pattern. But there's more to be done. We have to work on a change of heart and look at what circumstances, attitudes, and other behaviors contribute to the pattern. If we are self-indulgent with food, sex, or attention-seeking behaviors and do not ask ourselves, *What's missing for me that I need to fill it with this?* then simply choosing to stop the pattern won't last long. Lasting healing needs the practice of penance.

Putting It All Together, Alone and with Others

The words of St. Augustine place us in the right spirit for Lent:

O Lord, our Lord, you have created us for yourself, and our hearts are restless until they rest in you.

Lent is indeed how God draws us home as individuals, but it is also a very communal journey. We never journey alone, no matter how lonely we may feel. We are always journeying together. If we can experience our journey in communion with others, it makes it so much clearer that we are on a journey together. When we can share our experiences with a close friend or our worship community, we can enjoy support that allows grace to flourish.

Let us pray for one another on this journey, especially for those who need and desire a change of heart on this pilgrimage to Easter joy.

Choosing and acting Lent are so important because we are body-persons. We experience things with our senses, relish them with our imaginations, and we share in God's own creative and loving activity when our hearts and hands work together for and with others.

In the chapters that follow, we discuss a variety of choices and acts that have proved useful in our Lenten journey. Our discussion is hardly exhaustive. There are countless ways to experience Lent. They will come to mind as we continue to reflect on the question *What might I do, Lord, to grow in my appreciation of your love and my desire to share it with others?*

4

Realigning Our Priorities

At the Heart of Change Is an Examination of Our Priorities

All of us have named certain things as our priorities. From time to time, when we become aware of our neglecting something important, we say, "I have to make that a priority." Lent is a time for a top-to-bottom review of our priorities, examining what we value and what we actually do in our everyday lives.

Whenever we do this, we always discover that something needs realigning. We discover that there are values we hold, commitments we've made, growth we desire, that simply don't make it on the list of our "actual" priorities—that is, the things that take the first place in our lives. For example, we might say, "My family is my first priority," or "My faith is among my top priorities." But an honest examination of how we spend our time may show otherwise. We may say that we hear the words of Jesus that we will be judged on only one thing: how we care for the least of his sisters and brothers, but we may realize that feeding, clothing, caring for, or defending the marginal never makes it to our priority list.

A thorough review of what is most important to us and how we spend our time is prime Lenten activity. If what we are hoping to do during Lent is grow in personal freedom from our growing sense of God's love for us, our clearer vision of who we are, and our deepening desire to be more closely aligned with the heart of Jesus, then we will want to do this personal review very carefully. How else might we ever hope to achieve heroic, courageous, self-sacrificing service for others? What chance will caring for the poor ever have of making it into our priorities? How will we ever be able to break old, self-defeating habits and secure the establishment of new ones that help us be who we want to actually be?

Getting Started

We can start in a variety of ways, but it would be wonderful if we could start with prayer. We can ask God—in our own words and with desire—for the grace to do this review with honesty and with a desire to grow in freedom and integrity.

Who Am I? What Is My Purpose?

Then, I might want to spend a few days reflecting on the questions *Who am I?* and *What is my purpose?* Then, I might spend a few more days reflecting on who I say Jesus is, and what this means for me. It doesn't make sense to start with a review of what we value if we haven't first examined whether our values fit the truth of who we are and who we are called to be.

Naming Our Values

We then can name what is most important to us. It can be very helpful to write down these reflections on paper, editing and refining the words as we go along. Try to be as explicit as possible. Instead of saying, "My kids," spell out the values that are important in that statement. For example, "It is extremely important to me that I be there for and with my kids when they are encountering key growth moments in their lives, in so many areas—homework time, reflection time, in relationship struggles, in wins and losses, in relaxing and having fun." We want to open up our values as we name them. What does it mean to say that we value our faith or our relationship with God or service to others?

Spelling Out the Values in Actions

For each value, make a list of how that value translates into concrete behavior. For example, consider this wonderful value statement: "My relationship with my wife is the most important relationship of my life. I need her for my faith, and for my everyday strength. I want to be there for her, supporting her faith, affirming her, and caring for her in all her needs; I want to spend the rest of my life growing together in service of others."

The real work of choosing priorities happens when we spell out in actions what will give life to a value. The true test of a value's importance is how it survives, in competition with other important values, in the contest for time in our everyday life. We can tell what we really value by what we really do. When we feel like we're not doing what we really value, then we need to realign our priorities.

Be Complete

One of the serious mistakes in trying to realign priorities is overlooking things we might not be too aware of or about which we might not be too proud. If we're going to rearrange priorities—moving some things higher up on the list and others things lower down—then we need a complete list. There probably are things in our lives that we just do regularly: I read the paper every morning at six, go out to dinner every Saturday night; I have season tickets to a cultural or sports event. We need to name these activities. If watching a certain amount of television or watching a certain program every week is a priority, we should name it. If escaping into sexual fantasy is a quite regular thing, we should name it. Smoking, drinking, surfing the Internet, collecting ceramics, fixing up the basement—all of these are things that can become engaging, are often time and resource consuming, and should be named.

Establishing New Priorities

When all of our priorities are lined up like this, we are ready to revalue them. We don't want to rush this part of the process. Perhaps we can discuss this review with some of the people who are intimately involved with the choices we will make. And we will want to assess whether we have the freedom and grace we need to make the decisions we want to make and to begin to establish new patterns. That is precisely when it is important to turn to God with fresh desires, trusting that they have been inspired by God's initiative already, and ask for what we need.

The next step is to name first priorities. This may sound paradoxical: how many "first" priorities can I have? In this sense, my first priorities are the things that I will always do. In any competition for time, these choices win out, and that is what makes them first priorities. My relationship with God, with my family, with my faith community, with my friends, or with others in need might be in this category. This is what I do not want to neglect anymore.

Then we can name other important values, ones we don't want to neglect but want to distinguish from our first priorities. For example, these might be work priorities. They are very important, but we would realign them so that the first priorities actually come first.

Here is where the process of reevaluation gets to be purifying. I may discover that I spend more money on smoking, recreation, or knickknacks than I give in support of my faith community or the poor. I may realize that I spend more time watching television than praying. I may find it difficult to surrender something I "always do" for something I now want to make sure I always do. Because this is where we may need the most grace, this is a very important time to turn to the Lord and ask for help and freedom. Dying to self in order to be who we are called to be for and with others is not easy at first. With practice, it can become a source of great joy and fulfillment. With God's grace, it will be part of our contribution to the closeness of God's kingdom.

Building In a Review Time

Because realignment takes practice, it at times involves some backsliding. During a crisis or under pressure, our new priorities can vanish and we'll return to our old behaviors. That is why it is critical to keep reviewing how we are doing. During this Lenten time, we may build in a daily examination of how we are doing. Eventually, we may want to develop the practice of reviewing our day-to-day fidelity to our priorities every Sunday morning or some other time during the week. With each examination, we need to give thanks to God for the grace that has inspired and sustained this life-giving realignment of our priorities.

5

Lent in the Home

Lent is lived and practiced at home. Home is where we live out our various relationships. It is where we can take advantage of symbols that offer vitality to our religious experience. It is at home where we have accumulated many things and the patterns those things represent. It is at home where family prayer sustains us.

Family Conversion, Relationship Conversion

Lent is a good time to reflect on the people who mean the most to us and the relationships we hold most dear. For too many of us, it can be jarring to realize that our time together as a family might amount to no more than a few minutes a day. We scatter in different directions each day for work, school, or child care.

This season of reflection and renewal is an appropriate time to pray about our family life and how we can be more thoughtful and prayerful about Lent as a family.

We might hold a family meeting over dinner or some other relaxed time to discuss praying Lent as a family. We could discuss the symbols of Lent using the resources here and talk about how our faith life is not a journey we make alone but one we are in as a community, as a family.

A Lenten family practice might include a daily act of love for our family. Can we look around and see some small thing that needs to be done to make our lives together better? Is there laundry to sort or dishes to be washed? Is there a floor that needs sweeping or a room that needs dusting? Just one effort by each family member each day can make a dramatic difference in sharing the workload in the family. The grace we are seeking goes beyond satisfying the practical needs of the family. For example, we want to experience taking the garbage out as an act of love, an act of solidarity as a family. Perhaps the simplest way to prepare for this grace is to pray:

Dear Lord, may this simple, ordinary sacrifice of my time for the sake of those I love, draw us closer together as a family, whose hearts you are drawing to yourself in the togetherness of our family love.

Some of the real graces of Lent are forgiveness and reconciliation—mercy and healing. This is never simply a matter between Jesus and us as individuals. It always has something to do with family and relationships, with how we are with one another.

What in us needs mercy and healing? What patterns have we developed that need our reflections and common family choices and actions this Lent?

Symbols in the Home

We need to choose to let our homes be places full of the holy, full of things that help raise our minds and hearts to God. Our world is full of images that lure our minds and hearts elsewhere. Here are some symbols that will carry the ongoing meaning we give them, for us and for our families and loved ones.

Crucifix

Many of us probably have a crucifix in our home. If not, Lent is a wonderful time to buy one and place it in a central location. Even a child's drawing of Jesus' death can be a powerful, stirring reminder of God's love.

Water

A simple bowl of water, in a special place, can be transformed into an ongoing reminder of our journey to the font of baptism for the renewal of our commitment and life in Christ. We can pray, "Lord, may this water remind us of our baptism and be a blessing for our home, where our dying and rising in you is lived each day. Bless us, as we sign ourselves with it today."

Sand

A bowl of sand can help us remember our journey. God led the people in their journey in the desert. Jesus himself reenacted that journey to face his own temptations. The desert can be a place of retreat, where there is freedom from distractions. It can be a good place to be led and to face our temptations.

A Candle

A candle in a central place in our home can become the focus of prayer. Imagine praying over it together as we begin Lent: "Lord, thank you for the gift of your Light in the midst of all darkness. Let this candle be a symbol of our faith in your presence among us." We can light this candle whenever we feel tempted away from the light of Jesus, when we are experiencing tension in our home, or whenever we need special graces. Imagine how powerful the lighting of the new fire will be at the Easter Vigil.

It can be meaningful to bring out baptismal candles given to us or to our children and lay them near our central candle. We can remember the words that were spoken at baptism: "Receive the Light of Christ. Keep this flame burning brightly."

We can take out our family's white baptismal garments and remember the words "See in the white garments you wear, the outward sign of your Christian dignity. Bring this garment unstained to the joys of everlasting life." They are a symbol of the priesthood in Jesus that we all share.

Bible

The word is so important for us during Lent. The prominent presence of a Bible in our home can represent for us our desire for God's word in our lives. Imagine feeling a new inspiration or a softening of our hearts or just a sense of God's love, and picking up that Bible and simply, reverently kissing it.

Are there other symbols that make our particular journey full of meaning and faith? Think of ways to appreciate them more deeply during Lent.

Spring Cleaning for Freedom

Many of us have accumulated much more than we need. Our stuff bursts from our closets, overflows our shelves, and clutters our lives. Lent is a wonderful time to deliberately release ourselves from the many things we own by cleaning out our closets and simplifying our lives in a prayerful and intentional way.

On one level, spring cleaning is simply ridding ourselves of things we don't need or the things that we hate to part with except that they are so out of style. Certainly, many of us have extra things or things we don't need that would be wonderful for others who can't afford to buy so many things.

But spring cleaning can have spiritual meaning as well. We can advance the journey into personal freedom by asking ourselves how much we really need. How many sweaters, jackets, sport shirts, dresses, shoes? How much jewelry? How much sporting equipment? How much electronic equipment? How many sets of silverware or dishes? How much of so many things that we have in our lives?

We can be as serious and go as deeply into this cleaning as we desire to find fruit. This is not about getting rid of what we don't need. This is different, more faith filled, and takes us into giving up good stuff—perhaps stuff to which we are attached—because we want to experience the exercise of freedom. We do this because we sense that we are not free in some areas that are tremendously important to us, important to our salvation, and growing in freedom from the things of our lives can be a great grace. This freedom will place us in greater solidarity with those who find such great happiness and joy in trusting in God while they have so much less than we can imagine.

What else might we do that fits with our circumstances and the needs around us and in the world?

Family Prayer

One of the real challenges that we too often find in our busy lives is finding time to be together as a family. It is especially difficult to find opportunities to pray together. If prayer, other than going to church on Sunday, hasn't been a family tradition, it can seem unnatural to introduce it as something we might do together as family. Here are a few possibilities—call them dreams—for praying as a family during Lent or at any other time of the year.

Prayer before Meals

Meals are a natural time to pray as a family. We can begin by simply saying, "Let's pray," or "Let's pause for a minute to give thanks." This can be a brief prayer. Brief prayer doesn't have to be without substance or power. It doesn't always have to happen after the food is on the table. For a change of pattern, we could gather everyone to the table for prayer, and then bring the food to the table.

We can begin with a prayer of thanksgiving:

> Lord, we thank you for the blessings of this day
> and for this time together as family.
> We thank you for this wonderful meal
> and for this hour we can share it.

We always begin with thanksgiving. The reasons we give for our gratitude can be specific and draw us into this prayer from our real place in this day. We can say that we are grateful for this Lenten journey, which offers us renewal and prepares us to celebrate Easter with greater freedom. We can thank God for being with us each of us today, while we were apart, and for being with us tonight. We can thank God for some special grace that has occurred today. We can take time to let each person name one or two things for which he or she is grateful.

> Help us to remember those who have so much less than we do. Bless us as a family. Help us to grow in love and care for one another. We ask you to comfort and give strength and peace to those who are sick or struggling in any way.

This prayer should be very specific to our family. We all have family and friends who are sick or in need. Perhaps one of us is going through a special challenge or difficulty. We can turn to God with our concerns about a crisis in our city or country or some part of the world. With practice, this brief moment will help us be mindful of our desire to turn to God in all our needs. It will help us grow in a sense of compassion and care for so many people. Again, we may want to take time to let each person name one or two prayers of petition.

We can also pray for God's blessing:

Bless us, O Lord, and these your gifts,
which we are about to receive from your bounty
through Christ our Lord. Amen.

These options are from the *Book of Common Prayer*:

Give us grateful hearts, our Father, for all thy mercies,
and make us mindful of the needs of others;
through Jesus Christ our Lord. Amen.

Bless, O Lord, thy gifts to our use and us to thy service;
for Christ's sake. Amen.

Blessed are you, O Lord God, King of the Universe, for
you give us food to sustain our lives and make our hearts
   glad;
through Jesus Christ our Lord. Amen.

For these and all his mercies, God's holy Name be blessed
and praised;
through Jesus Christ our Lord. Amen.

Praying at Other Times
There are many other times or occasions when we can develop
the habit of praying together. These examples might inspire
our own creative or spontaneous prayer.
   In the Morning: It can be quite transformative of our
family bonds, in faith, to pause very briefly to pray together
in the morning. This might be a spontaneous prayer, such
as while we are lying in bed with our spouse:

Lord, be with us today, or Dear, I ask the Lord to give you strength and peace today at your meeting.

When we are rushing around one another in the kitchen and grabbing breakfast, it can be wonderful to pause to pray and simply ask the Lord to be with each of us in what we are about to do.

In the Car: Many of us spend a fair amount of time in the car, often with other members of our family. It is nice to begin or end the trip with a brief prayer:

Bless our shopping trip tonight. Help us be grateful for the gifts you give us. May this food (or these clothes) help us be mindful of those who have so much less than we do.

Bless my daughter (or son, sister, brother) at practice today. Give her gratitude and delight in the gifts you have given her. Help her to do her best, to encourage others, and to learn what you offer her today.

Lord, as we go to our friends' home for dinner, we thank you for our friendship with them, and we ask you to bless this night with all the graces you might offer us in the care we have for one another; we ask this in Jesus' name.

Lord, as we drive to church, we thank you for our faith and for this chance to be together with our parish community; please allow us to hear your word, to give you thanks and praise, and to be nourished for the mission you give us this week.

Other Times: We can say brief prayers like this at so many special times. It can be very important to pray together while cleaning up or in preparation for guests coming for dinner or for an overnight slumber party. We might share the responsibility for designing the family prayer for special occasions: birthdays, anniversaries, the beginning and end of a school year, the beginning of a new endeavor. We may want to add some special prayer time if one of our family members is experiencing a time of anxiety or crisis. For example, if one of us is waiting for test results from the doctor, we might place a special candle on our dining room table and light it each evening as we remember that person in our prayer.

Simple Rituals

We can easily add gestures that bring powerful prayer to our family life. One of the simplest and most natural gestures is to trace a cross on a loved one's forehead. It speaks volumes to a young child when a parent gives him or her this sign of love and prayer. This ritual can be done every day, when leaving for the day, or at bedtime. It can be reserved for special prayers of blessing before a big event. It can also be a powerful, faith-filled ritual for a husband and wife, as part of an everyday pattern or at times of great intimacy to touch each other in blessing.

Praying for One Another

The most important part of family prayer is perhaps the easiest to overlook: how we hold one another up to the Lord. Even when we are not physically together as a praying family, we want to pray for one another. In reality, this means that we have a pattern of talking with the Lord every day about the people we love most dearly. They become part of our relationship with God. This aspect of family prayer is especially important for a married couple with young children or for a single parent or for families with children who have grown up and begun lives of their own. We may not share our faith with our spouse, and perhaps our spouse doesn't pray at all, but we can talk with the Lord about our spouse every day—sometimes asking for help, sometimes just expressing gratitude, and sometimes begging for the gift of faith for our spouse.

May our Lord bless our praying, especially at home, in the community of our family, in these days of Lent.

6

Hearing the Cry of the Poor during Lent

Each year, the season of Lent offers us a time of renewal. Usually, we take up this Lenten journey as the gift of personal renewal in terms of our relationship with the Lord. Our renewal becomes concrete when it comes down to self-denial, which allows us to live our faith more authentically. The alms we give help us express our gratitude and allow us to exercise generosity.

Lent is also a time to focus beyond ourselves. It is a time of renewal that God offers us to hear the cry of the poor and to grow in solidarity with them. Ultimately, this is spiritual renewal as well and helps us grow closer to our Lord, who tells us that if we wish to love him we must hear the cry of the poor and express that love as love for the least of our brothers and sisters.

How Can We Hear the Cry of the Poor?

Hearing the cry of the poor starts with desire and a few choices. If we recognize a desire to be more attentive to the poor and to grow in solidarity with them, then it is likely that this is a grace we have received. Many things may have happened to open us to this grace, but it is important to name it and welcome it. God has been offering us this grace for some time and perhaps is preparing us to receive it this Lent. If we don't feel this desire, we can ask for it. We can ask our Lord to help us grow in a desire to better hear the cry of those most in need.

Who are the poor? Who are most in need? Who are pushed to the margins of neglect and powerlessness? It doesn't take a great social analysis to come up with some immediate answers, locally in our own world and across the globe. Listening to the news is a beginning. Who is suffering? Who is tremendously burdened? Poverty doesn't always make the news, but being sensitive to the stories we do hear is a place to start.

The U.S. Jesuit provincial superiors named four major groups that are most deserving of our care in their document "A Meditation on Our Response to the Call of Christ": "forced migrants (refugees, migrant workers, the undocumented); inner city populations (racial minorities, the elderly, the homeless, the persistently poor); indigenous peoples at home and abroad; and the globally destitute, more than 800 million people who go to bed hungry each night." The document asked, "How can we ignore the fact that those most in need of our solidarity are those who suffer painful hardships? Their misery seems almost inescapable. Many are trapped in poverty. So limited are their opportunities, their poverty has become structurally entrenched. Their lives are severely diminished; their hopes are crushed by a persistent and oppressive poverty that denies to all but the boldest the basics of human dignity and the opportunity to live happy and fulfilled lives."

What Do I Do When I Begin to Hear the Cry of the Poor?

We tend to not think of the poor very much because it makes us sad or feel like we are unable to help. But if we reflect on the situation of the poor near us and around the world, then the poor will help us come to know God's special love for them. Lent is a good time for this reflection. In this reflection we will discover God's love for us because we will experience solidarity with the poor. We can become aware of how narrow our concerns are or how self-centered we have become. Reflecting on the situation of the poor will draw us closer to them, help us understand the mystery of radical dependence on God. Ultimately, our closeness with the poor during Lent will make us more Christlike, for he is the one who became completely one with us.

Our Service for and with the Poor

Practical service isn't out of our reach. In many reflective ways, we can make choices to act in solidarity with those for whom we desire to have a special care, and from whom we know we will learn much about faith and trust in God.

Very many people depend on our charity. We live in societies that do not provide for an equal distribution of our resources or offer means for growth in dignity and justice in attaining them. We might take some time to research how the poorest of the poor are cared for in our area. We might practice our generosity in preparing food, serving it ourselves, or sharing what we have with food pantries that offer daily survival to those in need. We might be inspired to go deeper. What graces might come to us if we were to go to a meal program and eat with and visit with the poor? What fears would we need to overcome? What could we learn if we ask how they are getting along or if we ask them about their faith? We might grow in courage to bring our children or friends to spend time with the poor. How might we return to our lives with greater freedom and trust? What else might we do that fits with our circumstances and the needs around us and in the world?

How Will Solidarity with the Poor Affect Our Lenten Prayer?

If we spend Lent reflecting on the situation of the poor, we will begin to pray differently. We not only will see their radical dependence on God but also will find ourselves turning to God on their behalf before we ask anything of God for ourselves. This kind of prayer purifies our prayer. It helps us pray with a renewed spirit. It frees us from so many of the demands we place on God, especially for things like comfort or success or just getting things our way. With the poor as our prayer companions, we can surrender more easily and ask God for what really matters—first on their behalf and then for ourselves. Our prayer for ourselves will become a prayer that we might be transformed to be better servants for others, especially conscious of those on the margins of society. It will ultimately lead us to ask the Lord to help us simplify our lifestyle. We will ask to be freed from our dependence on so many of the benefits of the unjust social structures of our world. Finally, it might lead us to ask for the courage to act against those unjust social structures, and even to dismantle them.

Hearing the cry of the poor during Lent starts with awareness. It continues on to growing solidarity and deeper compassion and transformative prayer.

7

Fasting and Abstinence

What does it mean to fast? To fast is to do without food in order to experience the effects of not eating. It also serves as a penance or a sacrifice to strengthen us. When we don't eat for even a little while, we get hungry. When we get hungry, we have a heightened sense of awareness. We have a sluggish feeling when we eat too much; when we fast, we have a feeling of alertness. Fasting is a wonderful exercise whenever we want to ask for an important grace from God. Our fasting does not earn God's attention, but by fasting, we clarify our thinking and our feeling. Fasting purifies us and prepares us to pray more deeply.

When Do We Fast?

Catholics are required to fast on only two days of the year: Ash Wednesday and Good Friday. On these days, fasting has a specific and limited meaning of eating only one full meal that day, with no food between meals. It is understood that two other meals, if one eats three meals a day, should not total one full meal. One might fast in a more complete way, such as by eating only a portion of a single meal.

Of course, anyone is free to fast at any other time that it is helpful for prayer and reflection. It is not recommended that anyone with impaired health fast in any way. It is also important for people who fast to drink enough fluids on a fast day.

What Does It Mean to Abstain?

To abstain is to avoid eating meat as an act of penance, an act of sacrifice, which helps us grow in freedom to make much bigger sacrifices. Because many people in this world cannot afford to eat meat, our abstaining from meat can place us in solidarity with the poor of the world. Of course it does not make sense to make the sacrifice of not eating meat and instead eat a wonderful meal of fish or vegetables that we might enjoy even more. Many people eat a vegetarian diet for a variety of reasons, and abstaining from meat is not difficult for them. Perhaps on all the Fridays of Lent, as well as abstaining from meat, we could eat a very simple nonmeat meal in solidarity with the poor of the world.

When Do We Abstain?

During Lent, Catholics in the United States abstain from meat on Ash Wednesday and on all the Fridays of Lent. They fast on Ash Wednesday and Good Friday.

To abstain from meat on Ash Wednesday and all the Fridays of Lent means to not eat meat on those days. It does not intend the omission of eggs or dairy products.

The required fast on Ash Wednesday and Good Friday involves eating only one full meal on those days. One or two smaller meals may be taken on those days but may not total one full meal. The required fast does not allow eating anything between meals.

All Catholics who have completed their fourteenth year are bound by the law of abstinence; all adults are bound by the law of fast up to the beginning of their sixtieth year.

Nevertheless, pastors and parents are to see to it that minors who are not bound by the law of fast and abstinence are educated in an authentic sense of penance. (Code of Canon Law, #1252)

What about Giving Up Something for Lent?

Many of us might remember giving up candy for Lent when we were children, and it seemed like a real sacrifice. As we grew up, it was often more difficult to decide what special thing to do to make Lent a special season, to get our attention and to prepare ourselves for deeper sacrifices. For some of us, it could be committing ourselves to give up judging others. For others, it could be giving up a bad habit we've developed. Still others will have different answers to the question *What will help me grow in freedom?*

For many of us, the choice may not be to give something up, but to add something to our daily lives during Lent. We may commit ourselves to extra prayer time. We may decide to do some service for the poor once a week during Lent. We may choose to increase our almsgiving to the poor, maybe by choosing not to go out to eat one night a week and giving that amount to the poor.

Whether fasting, abstaining, or doing other acts of penance, the whole desire we should have is to use these means to help us grow closer to our Lord and prepare ourselves, in the words of the first preface of Lent, "to celebrate the paschal mystery with minds and hearts renewed."

May our Lord bless us all on this journey ahead.

8

Cooking during Lent

Lent is a wonderful time to bring together our spirituality and meal preparation. Food is rich in symbolism. Each step of food preparation can be open to meaning. If we are cooking for our family, sharing the meal can become part of our Lenten prayer and ritual.

The Fridays of Lent

Each Friday of Lent is a day we abstain from meat altogether. This is intended to be a religious experience, and we need to explore it and prepare for it. Of course, many of us can't afford to eat meat every day, so avoiding meat might not be a sacrifice. Some of us are vegetarians and don't have meat in our diet at all. Others might really enjoy seafood or a fish fry on Fridays. In any case, for all of us, not eating meat on Friday for whatever reason allows us to have some taste of a religious experience that places us together with our sisters and brothers around the world. How meaningful and powerful the experience is depends on the choices we make to ensure that there is some sacrifice in our Lenten Fridays and how reflective we are about it.

Meatless in Penance and Solidarity

How can we make Lenten Fridays days of penance that give us some experience of solidarity with the truly hungry of the earth?

First, we remember that we are keeping these Fridays special, as the day our Lord gave himself for us, selflessly and completely. This is the day that commemorates the Friday that we call "Good Friday." This commemoration is not intended to be sad or artificially gloomy. These Fridays are to be days that touch us deeply because we remember we are incredibly loved and that we have been redeemed from the hold sin and death have had over our lives. These are days to look upon a crucifix and feel gratitude in our hearts. We can also feel freedom—freedom from our sin and death, and freedom to love and give of ourselves more generously. Our experience tells us that we can't or won't be self-sacrificing without this experience of gratitude and without spiritual freedom. The Fridays of Lent are a spiritual exercise to offer us both of these graces.

Second, we desire to make our Lenten journey not only with Jesus but also with the poor of the world. What does gratitude do if not help us to stand with and love our sisters and brothers who have so much less than we do? One way we can intentionally place ourselves with the poor of the earth is to prepare our meals on these Fridays in ways that let us share a communion with them. Then our penance and solidarity come together in a wonderful religious experience.

Cooking As Prayer

If prayer is raising our minds and hearts to God, then anything can be prayer. Preparing a meal can certainly be a wonderful prayer. If our cooking is for our family or others with whom we live or our friends, then it can also be a great act of love.

It starts, as always, with desire. While I'm putting on my apron, or getting out my equipment, I can begin by naming my desire for this time.

Dear Lord, as you nourish us with your love, let me prepare this nourishment with you at my side. Give me the joy of being creative and loving, self-sacrificing and generous. As part of my baptism and my priesthood, let me offer this meal as a religious experience for me and for my family. As I prepare, help me to contemplate the women of the campos, barrios, and villages around the world who are preparing meals today for their families—with great love, and with what they have. Thank you for your love. I now prepare to share it. Amen.

Of course, we can add many words that are special to our circumstances:

Let this meal nourish Pedro with your love. He is so full of tension and worry. I love him and deeply desire to offer him this meal as something different, and a sign of my care and our faith.

O Lord, Meg needs you so much these days. She seems so distracted and not herself. Through our prayer and the sharing of this meal, give her the security of your love. And through our faith in your dying and rising for us, help her place the difficulties she is experiencing at school into her relationship with you.

Imagine how different getting dinner together can be if we fill those early busy moments of preparation with prayer, naming our desires so explicitly.

Blessed are you, Lord God of all creation, for it is from your goodness that we have this food, and the graces you give us in preparing and sharing it.

Bless us O Lord, and these your gifts, which we are about to receive, through Christ our Lord. Amen.

Rice and Beans

One of the easiest and simplest meals that can place us in solidarity with many of the poor of the world is a meal of rice and beans. This meal is healthy, nourishing, and filling. Praying during the preparation and eating of such a meal, feeling humble and honored to share it with our sisters and brothers in so many countries, can be a great source of devotion for us and for our families. Preparing rice and beans is very simple.

Rice and Beans

- Dried beans, or canned beans
- Onion
- Garlic
- 1 part rice
- 2 parts water
- Salt

Soak a variety of dried beans overnight (itself a reflection of our dryness and our need for "living water" to be restored). Sauté onion and garlic in a pot. You can add many different ingredients for flavor, such as sliced hot or sweet peppers, olives, cilantro, diced tomatoes, or barley. Then add the beans and enough water to cover them. Bring to a boil and simmer for an hour. To make the rice, add one part rice, two parts water, and salt to a pot. Bring to a boil and then reduce to a simmer for twenty to forty minutes (depending on the type of rice used). To serve, pour the beans over a bed of rice.

Vegetable Broth

Vegetable broth is a wonderful way to add simplicity, health, and solidarity to our meals. Making vegetable broth involves a little bit of trial and error, but with the method described here, it can help us be more reflective in our food preparation.

The simplest way to make a flavorful broth is to use vegetable scraps. Some people use a large plastic sandwich bag or a plastic container with a lid to store scraps in the freezer until they are ready to be used.

Scraps can include potato peels, carrot tops and shavings, onion peels, broccoli stems, celery tops and strings, bell pepper tops, tough asparagus ends, green bean ends, and the central core of a cabbage. These are all things most of us just throw away. Add about twice as much water as there are vegetables, a bit of salt, and bring the mixture to a boil. Let simmer for about an hour, until all the vegetables have become very soft. Then pour the broth through a strainer. When cooled, broth can even be frozen for use later in various-sized containers.

Vegetable broth is a base for a number of wonderful, quick healthy soups. Just add some cooked rice, pasta, or egg noodles; a tablespoon of tomato paste; thinly sliced and sautéed onions; or some frozen vegetables or crushed tomatoes. Wash, rinse, and add red or black beans that have been soaked overnight or canned beans to the broth. Barley or lentils add another layer of flavor. You can drizzle a partially beaten egg into boiling broth for egg-drop soup, or further season the broth with garlic powder, grated ginger, or crushed red pepper.

A great variety of meals can be made with a white sauce with a vegetable broth base. You can use the following easy recipe as the basis for many meals.

White Sauce

- ¼ cup of vegetable oil
- 2 tablespoons of flour
- 2 cups of vegetable broth (or 1 cup of broth and 1 cup of milk for a creamier sauce)

In a ten- or twelve-inch frying pan, add the vegetable oil and sprinkle the flour on top of the oil. Stir the flour into the oil until it disappears, just clouding the oil. At low heat, slowly pour in the vegetable broth and raise the heat slowly to medium. As the sauce thickens, lower the heat and add more vegetable broth or water to thin. Stir constantly until the sauce is the consistency of gravy. To make a brown gravy, add in a meatless browning liquid such as Kitchen Bouquet.

You can add in many different ingredients to this sauce to season it. Some examples: Add Parmesan cheese to serve over egg noodles. Add canned clams, tuna, or imitation crab and mushrooms to serve over linguine. Stir in grated cheddar cheese, pour over elbow macaroni, and bake briefly for homemade macaroni and cheese. Pour the white sauce over thinly sliced raw potatoes, and cover and bake for an hour with cheeses, thinly sliced onions or garlic, or bread crumbs. Add sliced hard-boiled eggs to the sauce and serve over toast.

Praying with Broth

There is something very special about making food from scraps. It is not until we save and use what we would normally throw away that we realize what we really throw away. Cooking meals in this way can open up a place of deep reflection and solidarity with those in this world who have so much less than we do.

All it takes is reflection and prayer. Reflection can take us as deeply as we want to go. We may realize that we don't take the time to prepare food at all. We may realize that the resources we have so completely separate us from the experience of the truly poor of the world that we need reflection to choose to open our heart in a new way. Perhaps, as we peel potatoes or break the ends off of string beans, we can picture ourselves side by side with someone preparing food for his or her family. In many parts of the world, such scraps feed chickens or goats that might be the only source of eggs or milk for a family. We can reflect, *Can I imagine what she is thinking about, as a mother of a poor family prepares her meal? Is she praying? What does she say to the Lord? Can I imagine "listening in" on her faith and trust in God?*

With this kind of reflection, prayer becomes easy. I can ask the Lord to give me some experience of love for this person I'm imagining. I can ask for faith and trust. I can express deep gratitude for what I have, and deep sorrow for what I waste or take for granted. I can ask for many graces for my family or friends who will share in the meal we are making. And, I can savor the gift that is offered to us in the scraps I would have ordinarily thrown away.

When we pray our grace before meals, we can give thanks and praise to God not only for the blessings of the food that nourishes us in such a delicious, simple, healthy way but also for the gifted solidarity with the poor that we experience.

Stews

The recipes for stews that follow are examples of healthy meals that people have made for a long time. Many families grow the food they eat, and stews like these can be much more than meals. They are part of a culture, a way of life, a set of values.

Most of us will have to go to the store to purchase vegetables. Some of them might be unfamiliar. If we start with a great desire to let cooking draw us closer to the Lord and to those in need, then the preparation of these special meals can become a time of grace.

We offer these recipes as ways to add to our prayer and experience of solidarity with the poor during Lent. Of course, they can be used at any time during the year.

Ratatouille

- 1 eggplant
- 3 zucchini
- 3 yellow squash
- 5 or 6 plum tomatoes (or canned tomatoes)
- 2 bell peppers
- 1 medium onion
- 6 cloves of garlic
- 1 tablespoon each of basil and oregano
- ½ teaspoon of ground black pepper
- ½ teaspoon crushed red pepper (optional)
- 3 bay leaves
- Olive oil
- Parmesan cheese

Peel and cube the eggplant, zucchini and squash. Slice the tomatoes (or hand crush canned tomatoes). Remove tops and inner membranes from peppers, and cut into eighths. Slice onion, and then cut into quarters. With the flat side of knife, press down on the garlic cloves, remove the skin, and slice.

In a large soup pot, sauté the peppers in a small amount of olive oil. As they soften, add the onions and the garlic and sauté until the onions are transparent. Then add eggplant, zucchini, squash, tomatoes, and herbs. Add enough water to cover vegetables.

Cook over medium heat until the mixture begins to boil. Lower to a simmer and cook for one hour, stirring occasionally. Alternatively, pour the mixture into a casserole dish, cover, and bake at 350 degrees for forty-five minutes (remove the cover during the last fifteen minutes). Top with grated Parmesan cheese, and serve.

Freeze the leftovers for later or share them with a family member or friend who may be in need of a wonderfully prepared, home-cooked meal. This dish is full of flavor, easy to make, and can be adapted in a variety of ways.

Root Vegetable Stew

- 1 medium rutabaga
- 2 turnips
- 4 parsnips
- 2 carrots
- 3 celery stalks
- 1 onion
- 4 garlic cloves
- Salt, pepper, basil, and oregano to taste
- 2 tablespoons of tomato paste

Because root vegetables often are waxed for sale in grocery stores, peel the vegetables and cube them into spoon-sized pieces. (Because of the wax, don't save the peels to make vegetable broth.)

Chop and sauté the onions, celery, and garlic in a stewing pot. Add the seasonings and herbs to taste. Cover the mixture with water and add several more cups of water. Bring to a boil and cook on low for one hour. Add in the tomato paste and return to low heat for another hour. Add more seasoning to taste.

Add a little water to thin if needed or, for a thicker stew, remove some of the broth and let it cool. Slowly add the cooled broth to a bowl with three to four tablespoons of flour. Whisk the flour into the liquid and add to the stew, returning the mixture to a near boil and stirring as it thickens.

This recipe is also very good overnight in a slow cooker. Add all of the ingredients except the tomato paste to the cooker and cook on high for an hour. Then add tomato paste and reduce to low for six to eight hours.

To use this recipe to make a potpie, cook the ingredients for one hour on the stove, pour into a pie pan (with or without dough on the bottom), and cover with pie dough. Then bake for an hour in the oven at 350 degrees.

Blessed are you, for it is from your goodness that this produce comes from the earth.
I thank you for this time and the opportunity to try something new.
I know that you are working hard to help me change my patterns.
I know you want to show me new ways, feed me with your love and your call.
With this meal, let me abstain not just from meat but from all that is not good for me.
Place me in a greater solidarity of compassion, help me live close to the earth and to daily food.
Teach me the joy of simplicity and trust in you.
I receive and share these gifts of your bounty, through Christ our Lord.

Fish Soup

- ½ medium onion, chopped
- 3 celery stalks, chopped
- 2 medium potatoes, chopped
- 3 medium carrots, chopped

- ½ to ¾ of a pound of flounder or whitefish
- Salt and pepper

Fish soups are easy to make, and they are nutritious and an experience of solidarity in their simplicity. Sauté the onion and celery until softened. Add in potatoes and carrots. Add in the fish (cook with the bones in for a marvelous flavor). Cover with water and then add double that amount of water. Add salt and pepper. Cover and bring to a boil, then reduce to a simmer.

After about thirty minutes, you can remove the larger pieces of fish, break them apart (if they haven't fallen apart already), and return them to the soup. You can add cayenne pepper, soup noodles, or broad egg noodles. Then enjoy a soup that many people around the world might be making at the same time with what they net from the water.

Imitation Crab Cakes

- 1 pound of Alaskan pollack or imitation crab meat
- 1 medium onion, finely diced
- 2 cups of seasoned bread crumbs
- ½ cup of Parmesan cheese, grated
- 2 tablespoons of mayonnaise or salad dressing
- ½ teaspoon of dry mustard (or prepared mustard)
- Worcestershire sauce
- Cayenne pepper (optional)
- 2 eggs
- Vegetable oil
- Lemon juice

Sauce

- 1 cup of mayonnaise or salad dressing
- ½ teaspoon of dry mustard

- Worcestershire sauce
- 1 tablespoon of lemon juice
- Cayenne pepper (optional)

Pollack is a fish that is tasty on its own or in imitation crab. It is inexpensive, low in cholesterol, and available frozen. If using frozen pollack, thaw in warm water for fifteen to twenty minutes. Drain and cover with water in a saucepan to steam for fifteen to twenty minutes. Pour off the water and let the fish cool. In a large mixing bowl add onion, bread crumbs, and Parmesan cheese. Crumble the fish into the mixture. Add in mayonnaise, mustard (a couple of squirts if using prepared mustard), Worcestershire sauce, cayenne pepper, and eggs. Mix ingredients together.

Form the mixture into cakes about one inch thick and four inches across. Dredge both sides of each cake in bread crumbs, and lightly brown with a small amount of oil in a frying pan. Remove to a baking sheet.

Bake the imitation crab cakes in the oven at 375 degrees for thirty minutes. To make a simple accompanying sauce, mix together mayonnaise, mustard (a few squirts if using prepared mustard), a few shakes of Worcestershire sauce, lemon juice, and a dash of cayenne pepper.

This same dish can be made with five or six peeled and diced yellow squash and/or zucchini substituted for the pollack. Leftover cakes may be frozen or shared with friends or someone in need of a special meal.

Lord, thank you for your love and mercy. Thank you for the wonder of the variety of fish of the sea. Thank you for this small opportunity to experience your goodness. Thank you for this chance to let this meal be an expression of love for my family.

Please, Lord, place me in greater simplicity and let me rejoice in humble food.

Let me experience even small moments of solidarity with the people of this earth who work hard.

I ask these graces with faith in Jesus.

9

Helping Children with Lent

As parents of young children know, Lent can be difficult in comparison to the anticipation and excitement of preparing for Christmas. What can this season of conversion and preparation "to celebrate the paschal mystery with mind and heart renewed" mean for children?

For many of us, when we were growing up Lent meant giving up candy. That wasn't a bad way to introduce us to the notion of self-discipline, but simply giving up something for Lent without an explanation of spirituality can leave children dreading Lent more than looking forward to it.

The most important thing for children is that we as adults understand Lent and enter into it ourselves with real devotion and joy. If Lent makes its way into our home and into the conversations and practices that children see, they will naturally grow up in a culture that embraces Lent as a season of grace.

Symbols also are very important. Children need context; they need to explore and understand what we take for granted and sometimes forget. When we put something in a central place in our home and call attention to it, children will naturally ask why it is there and what it means. In their curiosity, they want to know what has changed and what difference it makes for them.

With family prayer it is important to let the story of our salvation enter the imaginations of our children. Telling stories helps fit it all together for children (and for us). For example, a bowl of water in a central place in our home is a wonderful entry point to the season of Lent for the whole family. What does this water remind us of? Our baptism. Lent is a time when we want to be renewed in our baptism. For children you can bring out their baptismal candles or garments, or even photos of their baptism, as a reminder of this.

Helping children connect with their baptism can help them understand that when the water was poured over their foreheads, or when they were immersed in the water, they were placed with Jesus for the rest of their lives. You might act out baptism with a doll to help children understand. We don't baptize the doll but it can help us imagine what it was like when we were baptized.

Why does water help us think that we are one with Jesus? Water is essential to life; we can't survive without it. The story of creation begins with the Spirit of God hovering over the dark waters until God said, "Let there be light!" The story of the exodus from Egypt tells how God led his people to safety and freedom through the Red Sea. When John the Baptist was baptizing people in the river Jordan to help them turn away from sin and live a good life, Jesus came and asked to be baptized too because he wanted to show that he was completely part of our lives on this earth. When the centurion pierced Jesus' side after he died on the cross for us, blood and water flowed from him as a sign of the sacraments he would give us. There are small fonts of water at the doors of every church to remind us of the baptismal font in which we were baptized. Each time we enter a church, we dip our hands in that water and sign ourselves with the cross of our salvation.

Older children can help younger children during Lent. We can schedule a family gathering each week during which we say a prayer and plan out what each person in the family can do in the upcoming week both to help the whole family and to help the poor. For example, each child can be assigned one small task to help out the family this week. It could be an ordinary household chore, or it could be to draw a symbol for our Lenten journey—a picture of the people crossing the Red Sea, Jesus' baptism, the child's baptism, sadness and happiness in the family.

We can have discussions at our family get-together about plans for eating during Lent. Avoiding meat on this day places us in solidarity with our brothers and sisters in our city, our country, and around the world who are poor. We can also get a sense of our relationship with the poor as a family if we connect our meals to savings that we can give to the poor. We might make a meal each week to bring to a meal program for the homeless in the area. Children can help make a big pot of chili or sloppy joes and come along to deliver it to the meal program. This kind of family Lenten practice can transform a child's experience of the special power of Lent.

The most important lesson children can learn is to make Lent a time to practice being more loving. Children are naturally loving, but they can get into bad habits of fighting with their brothers and sisters, being disobedient, or even talking back. Lent is a great time to build in special family practices that can also renew parents and other adult family members. Children will notice if part of our Lenten journey is to choose to fast from crabbiness or busyness and to spend more time with them. They will notice if we set the example by complimenting others in the family more, highlighting the good things we notice in them. If our family Lenten practice is to focus on being nicer, kinder, and more generous in helping one another, the children will take part in it. And if we fail on a given day, we can quickly apologize and ask for forgiveness. That way we model the penitential and reconciliatory behavior that is central to Lent.

During Lent, we can do many things that make a huge difference in our children's experience of Lent. All it takes is a commitment of time and some creativity. One possibility is to take twenty minutes, perhaps on a Friday in Lent, to go through the stations of the cross together as a family and describe them as we go. The point is not to frighten children with the terrible things that happened to Jesus but to help them understand that he went through all of this for us, so that we need not fear death, for we are going to live with him forever.

We can prepare for Sunday Mass by looking at the upcoming Sunday's Gospel together on Saturday. The more the story of the Gospel enters the children's imagination, the more they can gain from celebrating the Sunday liturgy with the family. It is a great idea sometime during the day on Sunday to talk about the homily in terms of how it relates to the family.

Finally, the most important days to prepare for with children are Holy Thursday, Good Friday, and Holy Saturday—the three days toward which Lent builds. We can make these days special in the home even if we do not all celebrate the liturgies in person at church.

On Holy Thursday, we can prepare a special meal to remember the meal Jesus had with his disciples the night before he died for us and how he gave us his body and blood that night. We can prepare lamb with pita bread and wine to share the Passover story with children. This connection with every Eucharist can be a memorable time for children. After supper, the family might wash one another's feet as an important ritual to experience. This might seem awkward or uncomfortable at first. It is supposed to. We can then talk about what the ritual means for us, linking it to the gift of the Eucharist, as we live out the example of self-giving love Jesus gave for us.

On Good Friday, we can plan to observe the day in many special ways. We can plan our meals carefully to explain fasting and abstinence. Without jeopardizing children's health, we can demonstrate fasting to them and explain that it is meant to make us more alert and hungry for God's gifts to us. The time between noon and three o'clock can be a particularly quiet and reflective time. We can read the Passion story—from John's Gospel—and add our own words here and there to fill out the story, and let children ask questions. We can pray our petitions for all of God's people. It is a wonderful time to do the stations of the cross together. It can also be a time to venerate the cross together by embracing or kissing a family crucifix.

We can make Holy Saturday a time of waiting. We can remember that it is the only day of the church year on which there is no liturgy. We are conscious all day of the memory of Jesus in the tomb. It is a day in which we can help children talk about the reality of death, and then explain to them the anticipation of new life. If we really reflect on that tomb, which held the body of Jesus, we can really understand the power of our Easter joy: that the tomb is empty forever.

In this spirit, every family can do something to make Lent special for children.

10

Reconciliation and Healing

Lent is a wonderful time to celebrate the reconciling love and the healing graces our Lord offers us. Like all religious experience, Lent takes preparation.

Preparing

Reconciliation is what *God* does. We prepare for it by opening ourselves up, by reflecting on the areas of darkness in our lives into which God so deeply desires to shine a light. It might begin with the simple question *Where might God be offering me forgiveness and healing?*

If my answer is, "I don't know," then I have some reflecting to do. I can examine my life—what I have done and what I have failed to do—and see what graces are offered me there.

Coming to genuine sorrow for our sins is difficult. We might think that anything that makes us feel bad about ourselves is something to be avoided at all costs. If we avoid guilty feelings, we ask God to rouse in us a sense of embarrassment, leading to deep sorrow, about any way that we may not have been faithful, honest, loving, selfless, or generous. We can look at our responsibilities as neighbors, employees, members of a parish or congregation, parents, spouses, sons, or daughters.

God will always shine light into these important parts of our lives to help us experience remorse and a genuine desire for forgiveness and healing. The point here is ultimately to not focus on ourselves. God always reveals us to ourselves so that we see our need for our Savior. The focus is on God's reconciling, healing love. As the first letter of John says, "God showed his love for us when he sent his only Son into the world to give us life. Real love isn't our love for God, but his love for us. God sent his Son to be the sacrifice by which our sins are forgiven" (4:9–10 CEV).

Some of us experience troubling guilt that comes from deep childhood trauma or a long-standing sense of shame. This may hinder our ability to feel good about ourselves at all, and therefore to be able to reflect on our sins, the ways we fail at loving. If this is so, we can still prepare for genuine reconciliation by trusting God's love for us and by remembering two truths. First, God's love is unconditional. It is not conditioned on our being good people, or overcoming something, or even being good at all. God just loves us. We are always precious in the eyes of God, who made us and desires to embrace us with the gift of complete freedom in everlasting life. Second, God knows everything, including what we are suffering and struggling with. It's a personal love: The God of all compassion understands *me* and loves *me*. My greatest sin—the place where I need the greatest sorrow and desire for forgiveness and healing—is my lack of trust in God's complete and unconditional love for me. We can be certain God deeply desires to offer us this gift of love.

We might be intimidated by the size of the problem that comes to mind when we ask where God might be offering us forgiveness and healing. It might be a pattern of bad behavior toward our spouse and family. It might be our vices. I might say, "I feel sorry for how I treat my spouse or my children." I might focus on a long-established habit of self-indulgent sexual fantasy, internet pornography, or masturbation. We may feel remorse for all the good intentions that never make their way into action.

It is important not to stop there. No problem we have sums up all of who we are before God and others. The issues that come to mind might yield clues about some larger patterns. For example, I see that I tend to be loose with the truth at times. What does this reveal about me? I may discover that the real pattern of sin has to do with a deeper dishonesty or lack of integrity: hiding from God, leading a double life, not being who I really am called to be, trying to manage my life on my own terms, manipulating others for my own needs and desires. When the light of God's love shines into this level of self-awareness, I am touched by a powerful experience of reconciliation. Even here, in a place I might be most embarrassed and feel most naked, God is loving me and offering me wholeness and joy.

Celebrating Reconciliation

While reconciliation is what *God* does, receiving it and celebrating it are what *we* do. For Catholics, the sacrament of reconciliation is a most natural way to celebrate God's reconciliation. We used to think of this sacrament as only about confession—it was like a dumping ground for our sins where we were forgiven and had to pay a toll. One of the great recoveries in our Christian history is the rediscovery of the meaning of this sacrament.

It is God who forgives sins. God forgives us the very moment we realize we need forgiveness, which itself comes through God's grace. At that moment, we feel sorrow and a desire for forgiveness and healing, and we are reconciled with God. The reunion, the bond, the connection, and the joy are all there. Three more things remain: forgiveness and healing deep within our heart, celebration of that forgiveness, and participation in the healing process.

When I experience God's forgiveness and love, I am touched deeply. Experiencing compassion, patience, understanding, and forgiveness is itself transforming. If I fail to appreciate what I have just received freely and undeservedly, then I will take it for granted and risk moving on without real healing.

We need to celebrate the reconciliation we have received. In the sacrament of reconciliation—individually or in common—we have the wonderful opportunity to ritualize that celebration. In the sacrament, our personal journey is joined with the mystery of God's saving love, as seen in the Scriptures and in God's desire to save us all. This is deeply personal. There, in ritual form, even if it is just us and the priest, we step forward and admit that we are sinners, express our sorrow, and name the places in our life where God is shining a light into what we have done and what we have failed to do. Then God's forgiveness is proclaimed out loud for us to hear and rejoice in: "May God give you pardon and peace."

Part of the sacrament of reconciliation is healing. Often that will simply be prayer. Often expressing our gratitude to God is one of the most important steps on the road to recovery from our independence from God. Sometimes, we will need to practice a therapy that is more carefully focused on making choices about what I can practice doing and what I can practice avoiding.

May our Lord grant us all the gift of reconciliation, and may we all receive it and celebrate it well in the holy days ahead.

11

Getting Back on Track

What If at the Midpoint of Lent Not Much Is Going On?

We may think, *I began with the best of intentions, but I am not sure what I'm doing or what I want to be doing. Can my Lent be rescued?* Can a six-week journey be completed in the remaining two or three weeks? Of course, the answer is yes. It doesn't take long for God when we are ready.

How to Begin Again

If we have the desire for something real during Lent, the first step to beginning again has already begun. A therapist once said, "We get better when we get tired of not being better." This isn't the same as guilt. Feeling guilty for not doing much about Lent won't get us very far. What we need is a real desire—a real sense of expectation that God has something for us to hear, to learn, to change. We want to be ready to listen.

This desire can coexist with fear, with resistance, with bad habits that have been obstacles in the past. God doesn't need much of an opening to begin to free us and show us a transforming love.

A Little Desire Is Enough to Shape Deeper Desires

Once we can say that we want to make something of the precious days remaining in Lent, then we can start naming some more specific desires.

For some of us, it is obvious: a big, glaring, self-defeating pattern that stares us in the face. Most of the time, however, it takes a little reflection, a bit of honest examination of our conscience to see what is getting in the way of being a follower of Jesus.

After some reflection, we might admit that a streak of stubbornness, impatience, or harshness keeps putting us at odds with people. Perhaps an old wound or a fresh experience of hurt or loss has turned into a festering anger that robs us of simple joys and sorrows or compassion for the suffering of others. Maybe we are obsessed with how we appear to others, and our choices each day are guided by what will make other people like us. Our mood might change according to other people's response to us. We might see that we are compensating for some emptiness, loneliness, sadness, or insecurity by trying to fill in what is missing with temporary satisfaction, such as overeating, drinking too much, or escaping in sexual fantasy. We might be in conflict with our spouse because he or she won't do what we want, so we refuse to love generously. Or we might be punishing each other. Maybe a homily or something we read recently made us realize that we have not paid attention to the needs of the poor—and perhaps we've even taken stands and voted against issues or candidates who stand on the side of the poor. After some reflection, we may realize that we are not very grateful for what has been given to us and, therefore, we're just not very happy, generous, or free.

Lent Begins When We Say, "Help Me, Lord!"

With this kind of understanding, we can turn to the Lord with some real, concrete desires. Now we can wake up each morning and name a desire. While taking a shower or getting dressed in the morning we can say something like, "Lord, it feels so good to be honest with myself before you. Let me know your presence today. Help me face the challenges that will be there today. Give me some more freedom to make different choices and act on the graces you are giving me. Help me to refrain from escaping, but rather to give myself to loving, as you have loved me."

Short prayers like these shape our day! With these desires to let God's grace transform us, we can pause before going to bed each night and look back through the day to thank God for the places we felt God's presence and help.

Focusing Lent with a Plan

If we have a plan, we are more likely to follow it. That plan can have the following elements, which will give real purpose in vitality to our Lenten experience.

What Am I Going to Give Up Each Day?

What will we fast from, abstain from, every day? For most of us, whenever we feel the temptation to fall into a bad pattern, we will recognize it quickly and refrain from doing it. It is basically training in self-discipline for the purpose of letting God's grace have a chance to work in us. If we struggle with being crabby or impatient with various people throughout the day, then each morning we can ask for the grace to give that up today. We can practice some response that will replace it. Perhaps we will try to see other people the way God sees them. Perhaps we will imagine some pain, struggle, or insecurity in them that could be the reason they are annoying us. Perhaps we just need to say something affirming or complimentary to them. If we are tempted to escape in fantasy throughout the day, we can ask for the grace each morning to live with and embrace the real human beings we live with today.

How Can I Be Generous Today?

Almsgiving has been such an important part of Lent. For most of us it involves being more generous to the poor. For some of us, it means giving money to the poor for the first time. For others, it may be the time to prepare food for a meal program in our city. For some of us, it could mean simplifying our food or entertainment expenses and giving the amount of money saved each week to the poor. It is all about rooting out selfishness and practicing generosity so that God can free us to be more comfortable with the graces of gratitude and generosity.

Let's give Lent a new start in the days ahead. God is offering us more than we can ask or imagine.

12

Looking at Marriage during Lent

Lent seems to be the ideal time to look at marriage. How does our Lenten journey shape what we are called to do in marriage?

A few decades ago, the word *obey* was removed from wedding vows and replaced with the promise to love, honor, and cherish each other. Many years later, the Jesuit philosopher John Kavanaugh lamented how much we had lost by dropping the word *obey* from wedding vows. He said that the root of the word *obey* simply means to put the needs of another ahead of our own.

Obedience in this context has nothing to do with dominating another, only with two people pledging to put the needs of the other ahead of their own. What a wonderful idea. It seems that this is exactly what we are called to do in a gospel-based marriage.

We are called by Jesus to be unselfish. During these weeks of Lent we can take some time to examine our marriage. Do we love as deeply as we had originally intended when we first made our vows? As unselfishly? Whether we've been married three years or thirty, this sacred season could be the start of a renewed relationship with our spouse, shaped by our experience of Lent.

Jesus invites us to put the needs of another ahead of our own. We can deepen our commitments in marriage and even change the dynamics within our relationships through unconditional love. In loving this way, we transform not only our spouses but also, more importantly, ourselves.

For those of us who are parents, we probably always put the needs of our children first, but what about our spouse's needs? We care for each other, but do we put the other's needs ahead of our own? Imagine how profoundly our marriages might change if we simply lived that vow for a while.

During Lent, we can make obeying the special focus of our lives. Instead of giving up chocolate, what if each day during Lent we asked for the grace to be more unselfish in our marriage? As a first step, what if tomorrow, before we got out of bed, we asked God to help us love our spouse more? To put the needs of our life partner ahead of our own?

Silencing Our Disappointments

This Lenten journey begins with prayer and moves into silence. We hold off on the sarcastic comments aimed at our spouse. We silence a cutting remark, drop the correction before it comes out of our mouths, neglect the pouting, stop the stony silence when we are displeased. These behaviors can be long standing and not easy to change. It might take a while before our spouse really trusts our efforts. We will be the ones doing the giving for a while.

We are born selfish creatures crying out for someone to take care of our needs. The process of growing in this life seems to be learning how to become less selfish, less self-absorbed. On our good days, we can grow by loving, giving, and caring for others before thinking of ourselves. But on our bad days, we look at our spouses and others and grumble about the unfairness: "Why is it always me who has to do the giving? Why don't you (my spouse) have to care about me first? Am I always the one who has to apologize first? When is it my turn to be taken care of?"

We are called to love in marriage the way we are loved by Jesus—without figuring out what we will get out of it. "Love one another as I have loved you." *As I have loved you.* In the same way Jesus loves us—without limits. And so we love our spouse who is crabby and barking. Instead of snapping a response, we can ask ourselves, *What does my spouse need right now?* It's not about giving up our dignity or rolling over to a bully. None of this is intended to enable violence or abuse in unhealthy relationships, which need intervention or counseling. This is about loving someone who might not be very lovable right now.

We can wallow in our own self-pity and self-absorption, but it is in that moment that we are being called more deeply into Jesus' love. We must die to our own needs and our own longing in order to find a new life in Jesus. In a profound way, we are being called to the simplest task: to care about other people before we take care of ourselves. What kind of people would we be if we got everything we wanted? If we never had to move outside of our own needs and desires? Jesus asks us, "What good is it for us to get everything we want, if in the process we lose our very selves?"

Cherishing Each Other

We've stopped snapping back; we've held our complaints. Now, what if we add a small goal for ourselves every day? What if we perform one positive, loving act each day of Lent? We might hang up his clothes without complaining about it, or put the cap back on her toothpaste with a smile. We might lay out the crossword puzzle with a fresh pencil for him, or have a pot of coffee ready for her in the morning. We can do some of the tiny, thoughtful things we might have done years ago, before we slipped out of the habit.

It's not about spending money; it's a change of attention. Send him an e-mail of gratitude during the day. Tuck a note into her suitcase as she departs on a trip. Call just to say how grateful you are for having your spouse in your life. Each day we ask God for the grace to love as God loves us—without limits.

One final thing is patience. We have to learn to trust that eventually, with our constant loving and God's grace, our spouse will notice the difference. Under the barrage of love, our spouse will begin to soften, bark less, say "thank you" more. It takes time to change the patterns and time for our spouse to trust in the changes. It may take months beyond Lent, but if we believe in this, pray for it, and trust in God, the changes that happen in our marriages and ourselves can be dramatic.

This isn't something for wives to do for their husbands or husbands to do for their wives. It is what each of us as married people is called to do for the other. This is the way of life Jesus calls us to: "Whoever wishes to come after me must deny himself, take up his cross, and follow me" (Mark 8:34).

Refocusing our marriage invites us to be more giving, to fight our human nature that has us focused on our own needs. We are asked to stop keeping score with the ones we love and to put their needs ahead of our own. It is then, Jesus promises, that by losing our lives for his sake, we will find real life.

APPENDIX A

Lenten Gospels for Reflection

Three gospels from John are read on Sundays on the third, fourth, and fifth weeks of Lent. The Gospels used during Cycle A of the liturgical cycle are recommended at liturgies celebrating the Scrutinies of the Rite of Christian Initiation of Adults. Reflection on these gospels can help all of us prepare for Lent.

The Woman at the Well (John 4:3-42 NAB)

Jesus had to pass through Samaria. So he came to a town of Samaria called Sychar, near the plot of land that Jacob had given to his son Joseph. Jacob's well was there. Jesus, tired from his journey, sat down there at the well. It was about noon. A woman of Samaria came to draw water. Jesus said to her, "Give me a drink." His disciples had gone into the town to buy food. The Samaritan woman said to him, "How can you, a Jew, ask me, a Samaritan woman, for a drink?" (For Jews use nothing in common with Samaritans.) Jesus answered and said to her, "If you knew the gift of God and who is saying to you, 'Give me a drink,' you would have asked him and he would have given you living water." The woman said to him, "Sir, you do not even have a bucket and the cistern is deep; where then can you get this living water? Are you greater than our father Jacob, who gave us this cistern and drank from it himself with his children and his flocks?"

Jesus answered and said to her, "Everyone who drinks this water will be thirsty again; but whoever drinks the water I shall give will never thirst; the water I shall give will become in him a spring of water welling up to eternal life." The woman said to him, "Sir, give me this water, so that I may not be thirsty or have to keep coming here to draw water." Jesus said to her, "Go call your husband and come back." The woman answered and said to him, "I do not have a husband." Jesus answered her, "You are right in saying, 'I do not have a husband.' For you have had five husbands, and the one you have now is not your husband. What you have said is true."

The woman said to him, "Sir, I can see that you are a prophet. Our ancestors worshiped on this mountain; but you people say that the place to worship is in Jerusalem." Jesus said to her, "Believe me, woman, the hour is coming when you will worship the Father neither on this mountain nor in Jerusalem. You people worship what you do not understand; we worship what we understand, because salvation is from the Jews. But the hour is coming, and is now here, when true worshipers will worship the Father in Spirit and truth; and indeed the Father seeks such people to worship him. God is Spirit, and those who worship him must worship in Spirit and truth." The woman said to him, "I know that the Messiah is coming, the one called the Anointed; when he comes, he will tell us everything." Jesus said to her, "I am he, the one who is speaking with you."

At that moment his disciples returned, and were amazed that he was talking with a woman, but still no one said, "What are you looking for?" or "Why are you talking with her?" The woman left her water jar and went into the town and said to the people, "Come see a man who told me everything I have done. Could he possibly be the Messiah?" They went out of the town and came to him. Meanwhile, the disciples urged him, "Rabbi, eat." But he said to them, "I have food to eat of which you do not know." So the disciples said to one another, "Could someone have brought him something to eat?" Jesus said to them, "My food is to do the will of the one who sent me and to finish his work. Do you not say, 'In four months the harvest will be here'? I tell you, look up and see the fields ripe for the harvest. The reaper is already receiving his payment and gathering crops for eternal life, so that the sower and reaper can rejoice together. For here the saying is verified that 'One sows and another reaps.' I sent you to reap what you have not worked for; others have done the work, and you are sharing the fruits of their work."

Many of the Samaritans of that town began to believe in him because of the word of the woman who testified, "He told me everything I have done." When the Samaritans came to him, they invited him to stay with them; and he stayed there two days. Many more began to believe in him because of his word, and they said to the woman, "We no longer believe because of your word; for we have heard for ourselves, and we know that this is truly the savior of the world."

Reflection

Why did the Samaritan woman come to draw water at noon, the hottest time of the day?

What are the places in my life where I am embarrassed, where I avoid interaction with others?

What are the noonday wells of my life?

Imagine yourself as the woman in this passage. Jesus approaches you and tries to reveal his thirst to you—perhaps his thirst for intimacy with you—but you put him off. You are not worthy. It won't work. When he offers to satisfy your thirst, you put him off. You are convinced he can't satisfy your needs, at least not at this well and without a bucket.

Ask: How do I put Jesus off, with excuses, problems, or barriers? Examples might include saying, "I don't have time,"

"I haven't done this before," "My stuff is too complicated," or "I don't know how to find you in this mess."

When Jesus shows the woman that he knows her, she comes to understand she is in the presence of someone special—perhaps the One she has thirsted for all her life.

Do I let Jesus show me that he knows and understands me?

The grace will come when I see that I have been at the well a long time and have long been thirsty. When I can name the new thirst, the Water that now satisfies that thirst, I can overcome my remaining resistance to trust. When I see that Jesus reveals himself to me by revealing me to myself, thereby showing me my need for him as Savior, I will rejoice and tell the whole world, too.

The Man Born Blind (John 9:1-41 NAB)

As Jesus passed by he saw a man blind from birth.

His disciples asked him, "Rabbi, who sinned, this man or his parents, that he was born blind?" Jesus answered, "Neither he nor his parents sinned; it is so that the works of God might be made visible through him. We have to do the works of the one who sent me while it is day. Night is coming when no one can work. While I am in the world, I am the light of the world."

When he had said this, he spat on the ground and made clay with the saliva, and smeared the clay on his eyes, and said to him, "Go wash in the Pool of Siloam" (which means Sent). So he went and washed, and came back able to see. His neighbors and those who had seen him earlier as a beggar said, "Isn't this the one who used to sit and beg?" Some said, "It is," but others said, "No, he just looks like him." He said, "I am." So they said to him, "[So] how were your eyes opened?" He replied, "The man called Jesus made clay and anointed my eyes and told me, 'Go to Siloam and wash.' So I went there and washed and was able to see." And they said to him, "Where is he?" He said, "I don't know."

They brought the one who was once blind to the Pharisees. Now Jesus had made clay and opened his eyes on a sabbath. So then the Pharisees also asked him how he was able to see. He said to them, "He put clay on my eyes, and I washed, and now I can see." So some of the Pharisees said, "This man is not from God, because he does not keep the sabbath." [But] others said, "How can a sinful man do such signs?" And there was a division among them. So they said to the blind man again, "What do you have to say about him, since he opened your eyes?" He said, "He is a prophet." Now the Jews did not believe that he had been blind and gained his sight until they summoned the parents of the one who had gained his sight. They asked them, "Is this your son, who you say was born blind? How does he now see?" His parents answered and said, "We know that this is our son and that he was born blind. We do not know how he sees now, nor do we know who opened his eyes. Ask him, he is of age; he can speak for himself." His parents said this because they were afraid of the Jews, for the Jews had already agreed that if anyone acknowledged him as the Messiah, he would be expelled from the synagogue. For this reason his parents said, "He is of age; question him."

So a second time they called the man who had been blind and said to him, "Give God the praise! We know that this man is a sinner." He replied, "If he is a sinner, I do not know. One thing I do know is that I was blind and now I see." So they said to him, "What did he do to you? How did he open your eyes?" He answered them, "I told you already and you did not listen. Why do you want to hear it again? Do you want to become his disciples, too?" They ridiculed him and said, "You are that man's disciple; we are disciples of Moses! We know that God spoke to Moses, but we do not know where this one is from." The man answered and said to them,

"This is what is so amazing, that you do not know where he is from, yet he opened my eyes. We know that God does not listen to sinners, but if one is devout and does his will, he listens to him. It is unheard of that anyone ever opened the eyes of a person born blind. If this man were not from God, he would not be able to do anything." They answered and said to him, "You were born totally in sin, and are you trying to teach us?" Then they threw him out.

When Jesus heard that they had thrown him out, he found him and said, "Do you believe in the Son of Man?" He answered and said, "Who is he, sir, that I may believe in him?" Jesus said to him, "You have seen him and the one speaking with you is he." He said, "I do believe, Lord," and he worshiped him. Then Jesus said, "I came into this world for judgment, so that those who do not see might see, and those who do see might become blind." Some of the Pharisees who were with him heard this and said to him, "Surely we are not also blind, are we?" Jesus said to them, "If you were blind, you would have no sin; but now you are saying, 'We see,' so your sin remains."

Reflection
The man born blind washed the mud from his eyes in the pool called Siloam, which means "the one who is sent." How is Jesus a pool to wash the mud from your eyes so that you might see?

As soon as the man could see, his life became very difficult. People wondered whether he was the same man. Has the restoration of your sight so changed you that others are surprised at the transformation?

So much fear seems to surround the restoration of the man's sight. What fears do I now have about seeing clearly who Jesus is and what choices I must make to be with him?

The grace will come when I acknowledge that my eyes have been opened. Others may not want to believe I can see, but I know I can only keep repeating it, to myself and to them. I may experience rejection by some for claiming this new vision, but in the Light, I can see clearly the one who has healed me, and I give him thanks and praise.

The Raising of Lazarus (John 11:1-44 NAB)

Now a man was ill, Lazarus from Bethany, the village of Mary and her sister Martha. Mary was the one who had anointed the Lord with perfumed oil and dried his feet with her hair; it was her brother Lazarus who was ill. So the sisters sent word to Jesus, saying, "Master, the one you love is ill." When Jesus heard this he said, "This illness is not to end in death, but is for the glory of God, that the Son of God may be glorified through it." Now Jesus loved Martha and her sister and Lazarus. So when he heard that he was ill, he remained for two days in the place where he was. Then after this he said to his disciples, "Let us go back to Judea." The disciples said to him, "Rabbi, the Jews were just trying to stone you, and you want to go back there?" Jesus answered, "Are there not twelve hours in a day? If one walks during the day, he does not stumble, because he sees the light of this world. But if one walks at night, he stumbles, because the light is not in him." He said this, and then told them, "Our friend Lazarus is asleep, but I am going to awaken him." So the disciples said to him, "Master, if he is asleep, he will be saved." But Jesus was talking about his death, while they thought that he meant ordinary sleep. So then Jesus said to them clearly, "Lazarus has died. And I am glad for you that I was not there, that you may believe. Let us go to him." So Thomas, called Didymus, said to his fellow disciples, "Let us also go to die with him."

When Jesus arrived, he found that Lazarus had already been in the tomb for four days. Now Bethany was near Jerusalem, only about two miles away. And many of the Jews had come to Martha and Mary to comfort them about their brother. When

Martha heard that Jesus was coming, she went to meet him; but Mary sat at home. Martha said to Jesus, "Lord, if you had been here, my brother would not have died. [But] even now I know that whatever you ask of God, God will give you." Jesus said to her, "Your brother will rise." Martha said to him, "I know he will rise, in the resurrection on the last day." Jesus told her, "I am the resurrection and the life; whoever believes in me, even if he dies, will live, and everyone who lives and believes in me will never die. Do you believe this?" She said to him, "Yes, Lord. I have come to believe that you are the Messiah, the Son of God, the one who is coming into the world." When she had said this, she went and called her sister Mary secretly, saying, "The teacher is here and is asking for you." As soon as she heard this, she rose quickly and went to him. For Jesus had not yet come into the village, but was still where Martha had met him. So when the Jews who were with her in the house comforting her saw Mary get up quickly and go out, they followed her, presuming that she was going to the tomb to weep there. When Mary came to where Jesus was and saw him, she fell at his feet and said to him, "Lord, if you had been here, my brother would not have died." When Jesus saw her weeping and the Jews who had come with her weeping, he became perturbed and deeply troubled, and said, "Where have you laid him?" They said to him, "Sir, come and see." And Jesus wept. So the Jews said, "See how he loved him." But some of them said, "Could not the one who opened the eyes of the blind man have done something so that this man would not have died?"

So Jesus, perturbed again, came to the tomb. It was a cave, and a stone lay across it. Jesus said, "Take away the stone." Martha, the dead man's sister, said to him, "Lord, by now there will be a stench; he has been dead for four days." Jesus said to her, "Did I not tell you that if you believe you will see the glory of God?" So they took away the stone. And Jesus raised his eyes and said, "Father, I thank you for hearing me. I know that you always hear me; but because of the crowd here I have said this, that they may believe that you sent me." And when he had said this, he cried out in a loud voice, "Lazarus, come out!" The dead man came out, tied hand and foot with burial bands, and his face was wrapped in a cloth. So Jesus said to them, "Untie him and let him go."

Reflection
Martha speaks profound sorrow at the death of Lazarus, but it is tinged with blaming Jesus: "Lord, if you had been here, my brother would not have died."

Where do I resent the losses in my life and somehow blame God for them?

Even when Jesus tells Martha, "I am the one who raises the dead to life!" she finds it hard to believe. Where do I doubt that Jesus can bring life?

Jesus stands before the tomb weeping. He places no barriers to his feelings about death. Could he be staring at and facing the tomb of his own death? Can I be with him there? Can I stand before and face the tombs in my daily life?

Jesus shouts the liberating words of life, "Lazarus, come forth!" How is he shouting that to me today?

The grace will come when I experience how my "deaths" will not end in death but in giving glory to God. When I experience how entombed I have been, tied and bound, no longer alive, dead for a long time, I will sense the power of the command of Jesus that I "come forth."

A Mardi Gras Prayer

The Tuesday before Ash Wednesday is the last day of preparation for Lent. This day is known as Mardi Gras (or Fat Tuesday) and Carnival (which means, "farewell to meat") around the world, even where Lent has ceased to have much religious meaning. It is a festival, a last fling, before the prayerful fasting and abstinence of Lent.

We can give Mardi Gras some religious meaning by anticipating our fasting. We may go to a Mardi Gras party or visit a Carnival celebration with much feasting, or we may have a special family dinner together with meat. Whatever we do, we can let our feasting anticipate our fasting by beginning to focus on the meaning of the day when we first wake up. This can create a sense of anticipation all day that something new is about to begin tomorrow.

We can also prepare for whatever we will do, no matter how social or ordinary our day will be. Knowing why we go to a party, or enjoying the planning or preparation for a special meal, will add much meaning to this day.

In these or similar words, we can pray in the spirit of this day:

Blessed are you, Lord God of all creation, for it is from your goodness that we have this day to celebrate on the threshold of the Season of Lent.

Tomorrow we will fast and abstain from meat. Today we feast. We thank you for the abundance of gifts you shower upon us. We thank you especially for one another. As we give you thanks, we are mindful of those who have so much less than we do. As we share these wonderful gifts together, we commit ourselves to greater generosity toward those who need our support.

Prepare us for tomorrow. Tasting the fullness of what we have today, let us experience some hunger tomorrow. May our fasting make us more alert and may it heighten our consciousness so that we might be ready to hear your Word and respond to your call.

As our feasting fills us with gratitude, so may our fasting and abstinence hollow out in us a place for deeper desires and an attentiveness to hear the cry of the poor. May our self-denial turn our hearts to you and give us a new freedom for generous service to others.

We ask you these graces with our hearts full of delight and stirring with readiness for the journey ahead. We ask them with confidence in the name of Jesus the Lord.